PHARISEES BEHIND THE PULPIT

ELLIOTT BURNS

Edited by Keith Thomas Walker

KEITHWALKERBOOKS, INC
This is a UMS production

PHARISEES BEHIND THE PULPIT

KEITHWALKERBOOKS

Publishing Company
KeithWalkerBooks, Inc.
P.O. Box 331585
Fort Worth, TX 76163

All rights reserved. Except for use in any review, the reproduction or utilization of this manuscript in whole or partial in any form by any mechanical, electronic, or other means, not known or hereafter invented, including photocopying, xerography, and recording, or in any information retrieval or storage system, is forbidden without written permission of the publisher, KeithWalkerBooks, Inc.

For information write
KeithWalkerBooks, Inc.
P.O. Box 331585
Fort Worth, TX 76163

Copyright © 2012 Elliott Burns

ISBN-13 DIGIT: 978-0-9882180-2-4
ISBN-10 DIGIT: 098821802X
Manufactured in the United States of America

First Edition

Visit us at www.keithwalkerbooks.com

ACKNOWLEDGMENTS

First I must thank the Almighty and his son Yahusha Ha'Mashiach (Jesus Christ). I would also like to thank my beautiful wife Camelia, my mother Jo Ann Burns, my church family Chosen By God Ministries, and my publisher KeithWalkerBooks. I pray this book frees you and equips you with knowledge.

PHARISEES BEHIND THE PULPIT

FORWARD

BY KEITH THOMAS WALKER

This book started as a favor for a friend. I've known Elliott as a co-worker for more than five years. It's no secret that I've attained some success writing and later publishing books (mostly my own), so I'm constantly approached by writers who need help getting their book published.

When Elliott asked if I would publish a book for him, I told him, "Sure," with no hesitation, though at the time I no idea what type of book Elliott had written. I knew he was a spiritual man, and I assumed he'd written something along those lines. But in all honesty, I did not believe that Elliott would really produce a book. That's not a shot at Elliott. The fact is people ask me to help them with publishing or editing nearly every day. I tell them, "Okay, send me something," and that's the last I'll hear about it.

But Elliott did give me a book. I wasn't surprised that it was about religion, but I was surprised by the topic. Elliott is rather mild-mannered at our place of business, so I thought he'd write a guide for prayer or some type of Bible study. Instead Elliott gave me a book filled with controversy. It was about Pharisees, the evil they've been doing in the world, and why they're all destined for hell. Mr. Burns immediately had my attention.

I would consider myself an average guy. I'm no heavy sinner, but I'm not overly religious either. I do know a lot about the Bible, however, and I know that Pharisees are the people Jesus preached against in His time. Pharisees were the ones who prayed loudly and openly and were more interested in society's view of them rather than their actual relationship with God. I know that it was the Pharisees who were ultimately responsible for the Messiah's death.

In this book, Elliott reveals something that is rarely talked about today – something so abhorrent and widespread, masses upon masses of Christians might be headed for the gates of hell because of the very people they look to for guidance. In this book Elliott warns us that the Pharisees did not disappear in ancient times. They are still here, they live among us, and many of them are behind the church pulpit.

Now, if you're anything like me, you might want to roll your eyes at the idea of one pastor saying another pastor is wrong. You might want to defend your pastor – or all pastors – and try to shoot holes in this manuscript. That was my immediate reaction. Why should I (or anyone) listen to Elliott Burns? What makes him so right? Why should I even publish this book?

Regardless of how I feel about my pastor or Mr. Burns, the Bible is the bottom line. That's where all of the bickering stops. Elliott's beliefs are backed up by the word of God. This book is filled with scriptures that support his thinking.

Now, as a publisher, I don't necessarily have to believe in what an author like Mr. Burns is saying in order to publish his book. Whether his ideas will be accepted or not is totally up to the reader. But, for the record, I do believe that Mr. Burns is insightful. Everything he suggests to you in this book is backed up by scripture.

Fulfilling your spirituality is a personal journey, and it can be a touchy subject. Many scholars shy away from the topics in this book, but Mr. Burns tackles them head-on. He exposes the Pharisees who are still with us today, and Mr. Burns gives you the knowledge you need to spot the Pharisees in your own life.

If you find yourself in contention with any of the topics presented in this book, my advice for you is to simply read your Bible. Read the scriptures Mr. Burns directs you to, and read even more. Pharisees cannot pull the wool over the eyes of an educated Christian. This is something the Messiah taught his disciples over 2,000 ago, and it still holds true today.

Keith Thomas Walker

INTRODUCTION

This book is not to run down pious preachers denying the power thereof and stoning them with your mouths. There are good preachers and pastors who might simply be misled. But there are also pastors that the Bible calls brute beasts, *Jude 1:10*. Have you ever watched a cook with a carton of eggs? He or she does not man-handle them because they might break.

Under-shepherds should learn to handle God's people the same way. We should learn from Moses' mistake; when he called God's people a bunch of rebels and struck the rock twice, *Numbers 20:1-12*.

The Holy Spirit groomed me not just by His word, but also by allowing me to learn from other pastors and their fellowship. I have established good habits from some, however there are some assemblies that make you feel like you are in a horror flick.

My journey began when I attempted to help a pastor establish a church. Afterward, God's Spirit directed me to another church. Two years later the pastor died. It took the congregation two years to choose another, and things went downhill from there. I didn't know it at the time, but The Holy Spirit was showing me what not to do.

The purpose of this book is to set both lay members and pastors free from bondage by the power of God. Satan has used Pharisee and Sadducee spirits to run our assemblies with religious practices for too long. The Groomsman is coming for His bride sooner than we think.

To be honest, most believers are not ready, *Matthew 21:12-13*. Instead of a house of prayer, men have made their churches a den of thieves, and He's not happy about it. In this book, I will share my personal Pharisee experience, which I am sure many people of God can relate to. The Pharisees and Sadducees worked together to kill our Savior, and today they are still trying to kill the body of Christ though modern day preachers, *John 8:44*, *1 John 3:15*, *Matthew 3:7* and *Matthew 23:33*.

CHAPTER ONE
WHO ARE THE PHARISEES AND SADDUCEES?

The word Pharisee is Aramaic. It comes from *Daniel 5:28*, and it means "to separate." There were many popular Pharisees in the days of Christ. They believed the Jews had the power of revelation though oral traditions of the Torah and prophets. This is why you have to be careful with the Old Testament.

The Sadducees, however, had more political power. They observed written law, so they judged only from

Genesis through *Deuteronomy*. They did not believe in the rapture, nor did they teach casting out demons. They were more popular with the wealthy; the power players in Greece and Rome and with the Scribes.

I'm more concerned with the spiritual side of this, so I will discuss the politics later. To give you an example of a modern day Sadducee, I will discuss my interactions with a Jewish individual I spoke to on a regular basis. Concerned only with written law, he believed that his works would save him. He was void of love during his witnessing, and it was obvious that he was trying to prove a point instead of saving souls.

This individual believed that our sins were washed away before we became saved, and that God will not forgive us of anything thereafter. He went on to say that we can keep all 613 laws everyday without sinning. Mind you, we weren't arguing and he cursed twice during this conversation. From the Bible, I knew that cursing will expose your spirit, *James 3:10-13*.

I explained to him that it's not possible for man to live sin-free. As a matter of fact, you can sin with merely your thoughts, *Matthew 5:27-28*. I told him that no man can be saved by his works, *Ephesians 2:8-9*. I fear that my warning might have been in vain because this individual did not believe in the rapture. He was strong in the word, but he lacked revelation.

I do believe that we are descendants of Yisrael because overwhelming evidence supports this. But the word "Jew" is not found in the original manuscripts, nor is it found in the King James 1611 edition. The word Jew appeared in the 18th century, originating from Judea. But it is possible to convert to being a Jew. Judaism is a religion that

Christ did not practice, *Revelation 3:9* and *Revelation 2:9*. Christ was a Hebrew not a Jew. Why do you think they hated him?

Another example of a Pharisee is the Catholic Church. Like the Pharisees, the Roman Catholic Church has been known to add on or take away from God's laws or even change the context of scripture to alter the meaning. This phenomenon was even documented in *Roman Catholic Confessions for Protestants Oath, Article XI*: "We confess that the Pope has power of changing scripture and adding to it, and taking from it, according to his will."

According to Cardinal Gibbons, the Catholic Church even has power over the days of the week: "Sunday, it is the law of the Catholic Church alone," *American Sentinel, June 1893*. "The Sunday is purely a creation of the Catholic Church," *American Catholic Quarterly Review, January 1883*.

Of course the Bible contradicts all off that nonsense. According to *Hebrews 4:8-9*, "For if Yahusha had given them rest, and then would he not afterward have spoken of another, therefore keeping of Sabbath to the people of God." Don't take my word for it, look it up for yourselves. *Daniel 7:25* states the beast will "Speak against the Most High," and he will try to "change the set times and the law." It is clear that the Pharisees in the Catholic Church have been doing this for some time.

CHAPTER TWO
SADDUCEE SPIRIT

In Chapter 1 I spoke of a people who really think and teach like Sadducees, but spirits will change and they will pervert doctrines to make it look differently. But it's all the same. You can change its personality, but it's the same spirit.

When I was in an assembly where the pastor was called home, countless preachers tried to sway the assembly by literally almost preaching themselves to death. Sometimes I thought I would have to pull out an O2 tank to help them. They hooped and hollered, sang and sweated, causing the assembly to become excited. But then I noticed they had the word, but no true anointing.

The assembly wanted someone who had been to seminary. I noticed that most (but not all seminary preachers) were arrogant and full of themselves. Mind you, this was a Baptist assembly. Many of the pastors believed that simply because they had been to school, they were qualified.

Have you ever noticed preachers like this? They don't prophesize, lay hands, or show any kind of spiritual signs whatsoever. They're so prideful, they pervert the word "Reverend," *Psalm 111:9*. Preachers of this nature look down on smaller assemblies and demand that they get paid to work as a pastor. When they visit other churches, they request a huge amount of money, depending how famous they are, just to show up and preach. They avoid small ministries because those churches don't have the money they're looking for.

But the Bible teachers us that Paul was a tent maker. Peter was a fisherman, and they did not burden God's people, *1 Thessalonians 2:9*. And before you bring up the old adage about "muzzling an ox," let's look at why. To understand Paul in *1 Corinthians 9:13-14*, you have to go back to the Old Testament, *Numbers 18:21*, and you'll see that the tithes were food and shelter, not money.

Let's look at other examples. In the Old Testament, we see that the Levites earned their tithes because tending to the Tabernacle Tent was their job, *Deuteronomy 14:29*. In *Deuteronomy 26:12* we learn that the tithes belonged to the widows, the aged, the orphans and the homeless. The tithes were for the Levitical Priest, not the preachers.

Even in the New Testament, tithes weren't money, *Matthew 23:23* and

Luke 11:42. Have you ever noticed that when some assemblies prepare to collect tithes, they start their reading with *Malachi 3:8* instead of *Malachi 3:5*? That is because *Malachi 3:5* tells us who the tithes are truly for; the poor, the widows and the fatherless. Giving the tithes to the people in need is one religious practice we should have kept, *James 1:27*.

Now read *Hosea 4:1-6*. This portion of the Bible explains God's wrath for societies that lie and cheat and steal and don't show mercy and compassion to the less fortunate. This is why animals are mysteriously dying by the millions in our current society. If you don't keep the tithes pure, the nation is cursed. Remember, Abraham did not give Melchisedeck one red cent of anything he owned, *Hebrews 7:1, Genesis 14:16-17, Genesis 14:20-23*.

I find it odd how some preachers drive around with nice cars and live in huge houses while the widows in their assembly live from social security check to social security check. According to the word, the church's money belongs to them as well. Preachers like this are simply hustling God's people. Just because someone goes to seminary does not mean God called him them to preach nor does it automatically qualify them to be a pastor.

Which seminary did Moses go to become a pastor? Which school did King David go to? The fact is, many seminary pastors are full of knowledge but void of the truth and the Holy Spirit. There are some good seminarians out there, but from my experiences, they are few and far between.

I would like to close this chapter with a portion of my wife Camelia's testimony. These are her own words: About 11 years ago, I stopped going to church because I was deeply hurt by the church. I truly loved my Heavenly Father, and I wanted to be obedient to His word the way I was taught. Even though I didn't want to go to a church, I still wanted to pay my tithes and give my offering. At that time I was not working. I was receiving workman's compensation. I began to pray about it seriously, because I truly loved my Heavenly Father.

I felt the Holy Spirit nudging me. He began to speak to my spirit, and He told me, "SEND YOUR TITHES TO YOUR MOTHER." My father died in 1998, and my mother was receiving less than $800 a month to live on. Once I began to be obedient to the Holy Spirit and send her my tithes, I didn't want for anything.

I was a single mother raising three children, and I was receiving workman's comp. I didn't know all of the details in the Bible about how and when to tithe,

PHARISEES BEHIND THE PULPIT

but I assure you, I was blessed beyond measure. Obedience to the Heavenly Father is better than sacrifice, and it's better than listening to a worldly man.

CHAPTER THREE
THE PHARISEE SPIRIT

In Chapter One I spoke of those who hold the Pharisee's doctrines. Now let's look at the Pharisee spirit and how it jumps from one denomination to another.

Don't get me wrong, in Chapter Two I warned about seminary pastors, but I do think preachers should have some type of education. There are some preachers who believe that all they need is the Holy Spirit, but let's look at *John 14:26*. The Lord can't bring anything to your remembrance if you don't study the word first.

I find it interesting that musicians study their craft. Olympians train for hours, from sun up to sun down. But some radical, Holy-Spirit-filled-preachers, come up with a message on the spot. I believe this is why people often quote scriptures out of context.

One of the most misquoted scriptures is "Try the spirit by the spirit," but the Bible never said that, *1 John 4:1*. While I do believe in the spirit of discernment, discernment is not always spiritual, *Luke 12:56*. You can try a spirit by the word, but how can you try it if you have no word in you? While ignorance is more tolerable than arrogance, ignorance cannot be overlooked. Ignorance generally believes that the Ten Commandments have been or must be done away with, and that's just flat out not true. *Romans 7:12* teaches us that "Wherefore the law is holy, and the commandment holy, and just, and good."

This is similar to the Roman Catholic Church who tries to decide which laws we should keep and which ones we shouldn't. But the law is the law, *James 2:10*. This is why some say you should keep tithes but not the Sabbath. They tell you to honor your father and your mother (and your days will be long), but don't worry about dietary laws. Go ahead and eat unhealthy foods. It isn't going to kill you.

There are three things that I have noticed popping up in nearly every poor neighborhood: Liquor stores, loan companies and dialysis clinics. People have to be more careful about what we put into our body. *1 Timothy 4:4* tells us that everything God made is good and nothing is to be rejected. Unfortunately many people live by this until they literally die by it. Moses wrote about God's dietary laws in *Deuteronomy 14:3-21* and *Leviticus 11*. This is clearly scripture we should obey.

This is why it's so dangerous when we take the law out of context or allow the Pharisees to place their own moral and oral spin on the word. We as Christians must remember that the law itself cannot save us. We are saved by faith in Christ, and your faith will cause you to walk according to the law, *Galatians 3:12*. Don't take my word for it. Our Lord and Savior said in *John 14:15*, "If you love me keep my commandments." He did not say to simply "Keep my New Testament laws."

Many preachers put a lot of weight on the day of Pentecost but fail to realize that this was also the anniversary of God giving Moses the Ten Commandments, *Ezekiel 36:26* and *Ezekiel 11:19*. The Holy Spirit should cause you to search the scriptures – not just speak in tongues. These may seem like light matters, but eventually these preachers led to such doctrines as, "Once saved always saved," which causes millions to open their eyes in hell after they've breathed their last breath on earth.

Few realize that this doctrine actually came from slave owners. They lived with the notion that, I can beat, trap, steal, and kill you and still go to heaven. But God's word says we were meant to be free from sin, *Galatians 5:13*. *Galatians 5:19-21* teaches us that you also cannot indulge in idolatry, witchcraft, hatred or wrath and still make it to the Kingdom of God.

While it is true that no one can pluck us out of the Father's hand, we can choose to jump ship. There are Muslims and Jehovah Witnesses who were once Christians, *Matthew 7:21-23*. This is why the "Once saved, always saved" myth is so dangerous. People who preach this are also quick to tell you, "God knows my heart." They are correct, *Romans 10:9-10*. But your heart can change its mind. Just ask a divorcee how they feel about their ex-spouse.

It's sad to say, but sometimes people speak of God as if He's stupid. Trust me, He knows you really love clubbing more than Him. Love is and action word, *Mark 8:38*, so where are your works? Now read *Revelation 22:15*. The key word in this scripture is "dogs." And before your pastor tries to convince you that this scripture is only talking about false prophets, read *2 Peter 2:21-22*, *Deuteronomy 23:18* and *Philippians 3:2*. We must learn that the word "repent" means a lot more than simply asking for forgiveness. To fall into temptation is one thing, but to chase sin is another story.

I mentioned that Pharisee spirits often jump from one denomination to another. Just because you claim "non-denomination" does not mean you're safe from Pharisees. If you have a *Church of God in Christ* pastor, then that pastor will have a Church of God in Christ spirit. If the pastor is *Baptist*, then a Baptist spirit will be in the assembly, and so on. The sign on the church's door will not change the spirit of worship, but the pastor can.

    Speaking of worship, songs are very important, but you don't want to sound like you're at a funeral. You should have a balance of both praise and worship, *Ephesians 5:1*, *Colossians 3:16*. Remind the assembly that they are not at a club. I can't picture angels before God's throne doing the Electric Slide. Keep it Holy, for His Spirit is Holy. Stick to the word. It's one thing to be excited but another to mimic the Holy Spirit.

It's also important to pick a name for your church that fits your assembly. Even though a sign cannot change the spirit of worship, I do believe that names are very important. You should not name the assembly after a man, such as *Elder Chapel*, *Bishop Smith's Temple*, *Saint This* or *Saint That*. We are already sealed by God's name, *Revelation 7:3*.

Also, don't get caught up in clergy robes. The truth is the Apostles and Jesus were not Pharisees, and they did not dress up in priestly outfits. I am not a fan of clergy robes. The Catholics killed over 75 million people, so if it's distasteful to wear a swastika, then why is it not equally distasteful to wear a clergy robe? The Messiah gave us a strong indication that He's not a fan of them either in *Revelation 2:15*.

Everyone knows the Nicolaitans were an evil sect, but let's break down the word. Nicolaitan comes from two Greek words, "conqueror" and "people," which combines to mean conqueror of people. They were once disciples of Nicolas, *Acts 6:5*, but they strayed from the doctrine. There is another Greek word that comes from Nicolaitans. That word is "laity," which man gave the meaning "clergy." Therefore one could argue that "clergy" also means "conquer of people." Even though Jesus was not talking about the clergy collar itself, we must remember that *Revelation* was written for both past and present assemblies.

    Pastors are not more important than the people in their assembly, *Romans 2:11*. And if a pastor hates the doctrine, then why should he/she try so hard to look the part? A pastor carrying a Bible with five bodyguards flanking him looks too much like the Pharisees of the past.

I also take offense with religious assemblies referring to church leaders as "Father." Unfortunately this tradition is not limited to the Catholic Church. Even though Paul used the word "son" in *Philemon 1:10* and *Titus 1:4*, it was a figure of speech. We should call no religious figure "Father," for he can't create, only duplicate. When we claim someone as our Father in the ministry, we are claiming that the man birthed the ministry, but what does the word say in *Jeremiah 1:5*?

Rule number one: Do not duplicate another man's ministry. You are called to do what you are called to do, and you should be what Yahuah made you. Rule number two: When you claim someone as "Father," you're speaking their blessings and stumbling blocks over you. I have paid close attention to ministers who got caught up in embezzling and sexual scandals. Their father in the ministry had the same problems. You must always be careful about what you speak over yourself.

CHAPTER FOUR
PHARISEES WHORING WITH JEZEBEL

I agree with the scholars who believe that you must have witnessed Christ's resurrection to be called an Apostle. Paul believed this, too, *Corinthians 15:8-9*. Because he did not personally witnesses Jesus' resurrection, he felt that he was not worthy of such a title. So how can it be that there are new so-called "Apostles" popping up every day?

The problem is Pharisees continue to add doctrine to the Bible. When I first heard the words "Five Fold Ministry," it didn't sit right with my spirit.

Those words do not appear in the Bible. When you add titles to passages in the Bible, you can give people the wrong idea about the passage.

Soon after the Five Fold Ministry idea took hold, a whole army of "Apostles" began to appear. What was only meant as a statement became a doctrine. Let's look at *Ephesians 4:11*. We can all agree that the assembly is built on these five gifts: Apostles, prophets, evangelists, pastors and teachers. The key word is *gifts*.

Let's be honest; a pastor can only hold four gifts because he is not two different people. God gave us the five gifts to build His kingdom, not for an individual to build his church. This is not a chain of command. I repeat, this is not a chain of command! The largest assemblies I've been to had no Apostles. And anything with two heads is a monster.

Now let's digest the word "Jezebel." The Biblical character got her name from Be'el, which is another name for Satan. "Beelzebub" also means lord of flies. Be'el is also a root word of "Babel," which is a god from Babylon. Follow the history, and you'll see that Be'el is also another word for *lord*. This is why I'm careful to say, my Lord Yahuah or Yahusha because it's important to specify which "lord" you are faithful to.

The feminine meaning of Be'el is "lady mistress." This is why it's important to watch out for women who call themselves "Apostles" because they may feel they are lord over your assembly. In *Revelation 2:20* we are warned about "that woman Jezebel, which calleth herself a prophetess, to teach and to seduce my servants to commit fornication, and to eat things sacrificed unto idols."

Remember the confusion at the Tower of Babel? This confusion is still evident in assemblies today. The pastor says one thing. The "Apostle" says another. The pastor makes plans. The Apostle fibs on God and changes it. The under-shepherd only has one head shepherd. Any time two people try to drive one car, there is sure to be a wreck.

CHAPTER FIVE
THE GOVERNMENT AND RELIGION

For a long time in ancient Rome, the Sadducees were the ruling party, mainly because they had the rich and powerful members of Judean government backing them. Jerusalem was destroyed in 70 A.D. by the very people the Sadducees favored for their authority. This government involvement in religion made it possible for the Pharisees to take over.

Unfortunately the same is happening today. The dragon (better known as the government) will turn on all religion and Yahuah's people, *Revelation 12:17*. I believe they are already doing this with the help of tax forms such as the 501c3. Believers are being persecuted in America, but most don't realize it because this persecution is behind the scenes.

    Nearly every week I hear more stories of pastors going to jail and being fined for having worship in their homes. Not too long ago two pastors were arrested for praying on the lawn of the White House. And political correctness is getting more and more out of hand. I can call my African-American brothers and sisters the "N" word, but all hell breaks loose when someone refers to a homosexual as a "f-g." Many don't realize our freedom of speech is being impeded. How an under-shepherd directs the Head-Shepherd's people is between them. The government should have nothing to do with it!

I truly advise you to pray before filing tax forms such as the 501c3. Forms like this give the government too much power over your ministries. You should also be wary of government-issued preachers. They remind me of the Sadducees. It's clear they are the government's puppets. These appointed pastors preach too much about "Obeying the laws of the land" rather than reminding us about *Acts 5:29* which states, "We ought to obey God rather than man."

I'm not saying Yahusha won't keep the promise He made in *Revelation 3:10* ("Because thou hast kept the word of my patience, I also will keep thee from the hour of temptation, which shall come upon all the world"), but American Christians are living in La La Land if they believe that Egyptian, Kenyan, and Chinese Christians can suffer, but we can't.

People are always quoting scriptures out of context, preaching that, "We're not the children of wrath," *Ephesians 2:3*. Well, what about the church that was riddled with bullets in Kenya? They weren't the children of wrath either. People are fond of saying, "For God I live, and for God I die." Well, those words are about to be tested sooner than you think.

CHAPTER SIX
THE TRINITY

This part of the book is not for people who are weak in their faith. Just like the scene from the "Matrix" movie, you now have a choice. You can take the blue pill and forget you ever saw this book. Or you can take the red pill, and I will show you how deep the rabbit hole really goes.

Pastors and preachers are going to criticize me, saying "He's building his own kingdom," or "He's causing confusion," or "He's a synoptic." They'll say all sorts of things to keep you in bondage. But there is nothing at all sinister about me. I'm not a Branch Davidian with five wives. I have no sex slaves, and I've never preached that Christ had a wife or the Holy Spirit is a woman or anything else like that.

Remember, I'm only offering you the truth. I've offered scriptures and references for you to fact-check everything I've told you. Can your pastor say the same thing?

I had a vision recently. I saw a stone with three faces; a snake, a man and a lion. And then I saw the Bible. God led me to understand that The Father, The Son and the Holy Spirit are not one. He showed me examples in the Bible where The Father wills it, *Matthew 26:42*, The Son speaks it, *John 1:14*, and The Holy Spirit performs it, *Genesis 1:2*. He showed me more examples of how the Pharisees created the misguided *Trinity* doctrine and how they are still misleading assemblies today.

The word *sagent* is a Greek word meaning "net." God asked us to cast nets and gather Christians for his army, but Satan has placed a net inside Holy assemblies to gather more followers as well. I do believe the Bible is the breath of Yahuah, *2 Peter 1:21*. But Satan has used the errors of King James through ignorant preachers and Pharisees who refuse the truth.

Satan wants to mimic Yahuah's laws. He uses religious leaders and occult leaders to enforce his principles. There are two sets of Christians. The first group is of "The Way." This is because the word "Christian" did not exist in the days of Christ, and Jesus referred to himself as "the way," *John 14:6*.

The second group of Christians are those who follow Constantine's religion. These Christians celebrate Christmas and Easter. They participate in Early Sunrise and Sunday Worship. They also celebrate Valentine's Day, St. Patrick's Day, Halloween, Ash Wednesday and they put steeples on their buildings; basically everything Yahuah told us not to do.

Before I continue, I would like to remind you that it's not my intent to rile anyone up or fill them with thoughts of malice. It is not right to run white men down and kill them for something their forefathers did during the days of slavery. The same goes for the Catholic Church. There are good people in the Catholic assemblies. They are just in bondage. Pope John Paul II said, "Don't go to God for forgiveness of sins, come to me," *L.A. Times, December 12, 1984*. But the new covenant tells us Yahusha is our mediator, not the Pope, *1 Timothy 2:5*.

While I do believe in the Father, the Son and the Holy Spirit, Jesus and His Apostles did not teach the trinity doctrine. It is a fact that *1 John 5:7* ("For there are three that bear record in heaven, the Father, the word, and the Holy Ghost: and these three are one") was not included in the original manuscripts. It was added to the Bible afterwards, and it was translated from Latin, which means John most likely did not write it himself (the original manuscripts were written in Hebrew).

In 1522, Martin Luther wrote, "it is indeed true that the name Trinity is nowhere to be found in the Holy Scriptures, but has been conceived and invented by man." Other scholars believe that the original Greek manuscripts probably read, "For there are three that testify, the Spirit and the water and the blood, and these three are in agreement."

The trinity doctrine dates back to the days of Babylon. Constantine was a sun worshiper. The doctrine of the trinity was made official at the Council of Constantinople and was enforced by the Emperor Theodosius by punishment and even death. Between 1846 and 1888 most of the leading Adventist writers rejected the trinity. There was still no consensus at the Bible Conference of 1919. It is believed that Ellen White, a founder of the Seventh-day Adventist Church, was a major supporter of the trinity doctrine and is largely responsible for the teachings that continue today.

Man's definition of the trinity is a mystery. Is it three in one or one in three? But the word of God is not confused on this matter, *John 17:3*. Preachers can't explain the trinity because it's a man made doctrine. But the Bible's doctrine of the trinity is quite different and not a mystery to understand. Yahusha is subject to the Father's will, *John 17:4*.

Now read *Matthew 24:36* ("But of that day and hour knoweth no man, no, not the angels of heaven, but my Father only"). This is just one example of Jesus indicating he is not the same as His Father. Don't get me wrong, Yahusha embodies the Father's glory and authority, *Colossians 2:9*. But He is not the Father. He is under the Father's authority, *John 14:28*. The Holy Spirit is a separate entity as well.

CHAPTER SEVEN
WHO DO YOU WORSHIP? WHAT DO YOU CELEBRATE?

Throughout this book, you've heard me refer to God as Yahuah and his son as Yahusha. In this chapter I will explain why I use these names and why I believe referring to The Son as "Jesus" is inappropriate.

I'll be the first to admit that discovering The Son's real name is hard work, but it's worth the research. In *Zachariah 3:8*, Christ is referred to as "Joshua," which was translated from "Yeoshua." This is a hint to the savior's real name, but we must remember that there was more than one Joshua in the Bible. There was "Jehoshua" (Yeoshua) in *Numbers 13:16* and "Jeshua" (Yeshua) in *Nehemiah 8:17*.

We all know that God referred to Himself as "I AM," which translates to *Hayah* in Hebrew. "Yasha" is another Hebrew word that means salvation. In *John 5:43* Christ says, "I have come in my father's name." *Psalms 68:4* tells us to sing praises to God in his name, "JAH." But it's important to note that there was no letter "J" when the Bible was written.

Over 2000 times in the Old Testament (the original one, written in Hebrew) you find *Yah* and *Yahu* referring to the Father, therefore His name cannot be "*Yahweh*." Yahweh is missing the *u*, and the *w* did not exist in the Hebrew alphabet when the original manuscripts were written. The *w* was created to make the *uu* sound.

In Hebrew, when the vowels *YH* are together, it becomes *YAH* and *UH* becomes *UAH*. Put them together, and you get *Yahuah*. This is God's true name. The pronunciation is not as important as the meaning. The Son's name, *Yahusha*, means *I Am Salvation*. The Father's name, *Yahuah*, means *I Am Eternal, I Am Self Existing, Exodus 3:14*.

Why is it important to get Yahusha's name correct? I believe it's important because the anti-messiah will call himself "Jesus." He will teach that the Sabbath Day is for rest only and not a day of worship. "Iesous" is the Greek word for "Jesus." The numerical sum of the Greek letters in "Iesous" equals 888, which in turn means *useless*. Also the numerical sum of the word "Jesus" equals 666, which is the mark of the beast.

    The anti-Christ will also cause you to worship unholy holidays. Take Valentines' Day for example. This holiday originated from the story of Nimrod's wife-mother. Nimrod was Yahuah's enemy who led the tower of Babel, *Genesis 10:8-10*. Nimrod was the first king of Babylon. His wife-mother was jealous of other women because of Nimrod's handsomeness. Nimrod often carried a bow, and he is the "baby cupid" many Christians celebrate each February 14th. Nimrod was killed, and his body parts were spread around the land to show that he was human, not a god.

    Legend has it that Nimrod's arm fell in the water, and the fish god "Dagon" was born. Roman Catholic Priests wear the same hat as the Babylonian priests, which had a fish mouth on top.

So we must ask if those Pharisees are still worshipping the fish god.

It is also well known that ancient societies worshipped the sun god with monuments called *obelisks*. Constantine brought the sun worship to Rome, and thanks to him, your churches now have similar monuments called "steeples."

After Nimrod's death, his mother-wife had a son named Tammuz. She declared Tammuz was Nimrod reincarnated. As proof, she showed everyone an evergreen tree that sprung up virtually overnight on the night Tammuz was born. Throughout his life, Tammuz returned to the evergreen and placed gifts to mark the anniversary of his birth. This is how the present-day Christmas holiday came about.

Almost every so-called "Christian" holiday has roots to pagan holidays. Easter is another one that was inspired by Nimrod. His mother-wife (yes, he married his mother) later became Diana, the goddess of fertility. This is where we get Easter egg hunting from; many were hoping the sun god would be resurrected as an egg. Also the halo on the saints' pictures derived from sun worship.

Another word the Pharisees have corrupted is "Amen." Few people know that we should really say, "Amein." Amein means "so be it," or "verily-surely." Amein is in the *Strong's Concordance #543* and in the *Hebrew Lexicon #281*.

"Amen" is an Egyptian god, derived from amen-ra. Yahusha called himself "Amein" in *Revelation 3:14*. You should also note that Yahusha did not end His prayers in amen – nor does the book of Revelation end in amen. The word was put there by the translators. Nowhere in the Old Testament did the people end their prayers with amen.

Also, contrary to what Pharisees would have you believe, the word "ekklesia" does not mean "church." It literally translates to "meeting," or "gathering," not building. The word *church* was born in *Acts 19:37*, but it was used for pagan gatherings. The true meaning of "church" can be traced back to circe, circus or circle. Circe is the daughter of the sun god Helios. She is also known as Kirk. She's often pictured with a cup in her hand mixed with wine and drugs, *Revelation 17:4-6*.

Lastly, there is no such thing as Baptist faith, Catholic faith, Mormon faith, Pentecostal, COGIC, or anything like that. There is only one Faith, *Ephesians 4:5*. Today, the Pharisees may not cause people to worship false gods, but they do cause people to worship Yahuah falsely, *Matthew 15:8-9*.

I'm not saying everybody is going to hell for having Sunday service instead of on Saturday and calling on the name *Jesus*. But remember, Yahuah has a direct will and a submissive will, *Matthew 5:19*. You may not suffer, but the men who knew better and forced man's will over Yahuah's will, will suffer greatly, *Revelation 22:19, James 3:1*.

    Remember not to bow down to angel statues and Catholic men. Remember that cutting down trees, boiling eggs, painting them, hunting them and celebrating Halloween is all rooted in pagan celebrations.

    If you insist on calling Yahuah – Jehovah, Yahusha – Jesus and exchange the Sabbath for Sunday, that's fine. You have to answer to Yahuah for yourself. But if my pastor can't be honest and tell me the true name of Jesus, tell me who changed the Sabbath days, and he doesn't even know the name of the Father, then why should I trust him with my soul?

CHAPTER EIGHT
PHARISEES IN AMERICA

Even though Satan used the Vatican Bishops and Popes to push his agenda, I do believe America is the troubled nation the Bible refers to in *Revelation 18*.

I had a vision. I woke up and looked out of my window. Everything was different. I was different. I saw a crowd outside, so I went to see what was happening, and there I saw Jesus Christ. He had on a red robe. He had a bright face that shined. His feet were like brass. He had red eyes and dark, beautiful skin.

He spoke to the crowd. He said women should stop wearing short skirts or anything that shows their bodies as sex objects, tempting men. And Jesus said men should keep their hair short. People stood in amazement. They asked, "When are you coming back?" Jesus answered, "Very soon!"

As I stood in awe, the Messiah introduced himself as a human would. He shook my hand and said, "I am Jesus Christ. Come, follow me." He had a group of brothers with Him. And then I saw a woman. She was beautiful. She wore a red skirt. It was very short. As I watched her with lust, Christ's eyes pierced my soul, convicting me.

The woman started bragging about her men and her beauty, and this woman asked Jesus, "How many children will I have?" Jesus held up five fingers, and the woman yelled, "That many, that long." At that moment, I awakened from my vision.

Before I go any further, I would like to clear up any confusion you may have over my use of the name "Jesus" sometimes rather than "Yahusha." I do this for you, the reader. I have taught you the correct name of the Messiah, but I understand that you may still relate to Him better as "Jesus." I pray that you will eventually change your way of thinking, but salvation is not based solely on the pronunciation of His name.

I was only seventeen when I had the vision I just described, so I prayed for understanding. The Spirit led me to *Revelation 19:12-13* ("He had a name written, that no one knew, but himself. He was clothed with a vesture dipped in blood"). *Revelation 1:14-15* was also exactly like my vision: "His eyes were as a flame of fire. And his feet like unto fine brass."

I realized that the woman from my vision was the whore of Babylon. Rather than a number of children she would have, Christ's five fingers could be represented as years, or it could be our five most recent presidents. I now know that there are 44 kings of Israel in the Bible, and President Obama is our 44th president.

There are other prophecies that I've noticed recently. *Psalm 90:10* tells us our lifespan is 70 years. Is this referring to individuals or all of earth? Israel became a nation in 1948. Abraham was born 1948 years after Adam. Israel will be 70 years old in 2016. I know that there is no time clock in heaven, but that does not mean that Yahuah does not have earth on a time line. *2 Peter 3:8* tells us that He definitely does.

The truth is we are now in the "last days." Yahusha is now past the door post, *Matthew 24:33-34*. We currently have five main cults inside the Christian community; Jehovah Witnesses, Mormons, Catholics, Scientologists and Prosperity Healers. Women are showing off their bodies more and more these days. Men are wearing their hair long, sometimes even opting for feminine perms.

    Before someone calls me a doomsday preacher, please note that I am not trying to predict the date of the rapture. I am merely pointing out the obvious signs. Can you not hear the trumpet blast sounding from the sky? Do you not see the animals dying by the millions, all volcanoes in the world becoming active?

    God gave me a dream concerning the U.S. in its present state. I saw rivers with bad waters that stunk. I saw food in the grocery store with prices that were sky-high. I saw that foreigners owned all of our businesses. In my dream, God judged America like Sodom and Gomorrah. He judged those who committed sodomy, those who chose evil over good, the murderers and child molesters, the women perverts and the mockers. I saw news reports that were filled with gloom for America. There was fear of nuclear war. If you pay attention, you'll see that many of the things in my dream are already coming true.

Did you know there is a Stonehenge in America? It's called the "Georgia Guidestones." An unknown person (or persons) named "R.C. Christian" hired a granite company to erect it. The structure may have been built for Satanic purposes, and the worst thing is the stones have their own commandments – which appear to mimic the Ten Commandments. Here are the fake commandments that are written in many languages on the Georgia stones:

1. Maintain humanity five million with balance of nature
2. Guide reproduction wisely
3. Unite humanity with a living new language
4. Rule Passion-Faith-Tradition and all things tempered
5. Protect people and nations with fair laws and justice
6. Let all nations rule internally, resolving external disputes in a world court
7. Avoid petty laws and useless officials
8. Balance personal rights with social duties
9. Prize truth, beauty, loving and seeking harmony
10. Be not a cancer on the earth, leave room for nature

I know some of those rules seem innocent, but they are not. When you put a precise number on the amount of people who can exist on earth, for example, it will lead to murder and abortions. Uniting the world with one language sounds suspiciously like the New World Order. Who's to say what laws are petty and which officials are needed? And any commandment that tells you to "prize beauty" is definitely against the Bible.

Don't be surprised if America or the whole world makes these fake commandments law. Pharisees love to change the words of God to fit their own twisted agendas. If they can rewrite something as sacred as the Ten Commandments, where will it stop?

CHAPTER NINE
CHOSEN BY GOD MINISTRIES

I've learned that when you're evangelizing, it's important to speak to people in their language. Here's a perfect example.

One morning my wife went to the grocery store, and it started to rain. There was a woman going to the bus stop with her daughter and a buggy full of groceries. My wife Camelia offered her a ride, and she and the woman started talking.

My wife referred to our Heavenly father as "Yahweh" (this was before we knew any better). The woman was excited that Camelia knew the name Yah. She explained to my wife that she shared the name "Yah" with her parents and told them that the name "Jesus" was not real, and they told her she lost her mind.

Of course that woman's parents were out of line, but many preachers carry that same attitude. They are resistant to even saying "Yahusha." They know Jesus is a transliteration rather than a precise translation, but they are afraid of the truth. Some are so stubborn, you can't tell them anything.

I will share another Pharisee experience I had. God led me to a ministry. This is where I met my wife. Not long after I arrived at the assembly, Camelia and other members began to come to my home for Bible study. One of the church members who came to my home told the pastor about my Bible studies. The pastor showed himself to be a Pharisee the following Sunday. He acted a fool behind the pulpit, telling the congregation that we cannot have Bible study at our home anymore. Of course that order was ridiculous, and it went against the teachings in the Bible.

On another Sunday at the same assembly, my wife noticed this question in the Sunday school book: "How would you improve the spiritual growth in your church?" My wife went to the pastor and suggested we invest in more books. The pastor became angry again. He ranted and raved, saying, "I'm the pastor. You don't need those books. I hear from God!" This went on for several services.

Every Sunday after service, I would leave the assembly and walk to the park down the street to pray. Each time I prayed, the clouds would part, and the sun shone directly on me as I spoke in tongues.

My daughter-in-law told me about a dream she had. She saw me behind the pulpit preaching. She saw me walking through the church, banishing everyone, saying, "Get out, and get out now!" As the congregation fled, demons chased their cars. They looked back and saw that the church was in a graveyard, and demons engulfed the building.

When my wife and our family finally left the church, I went to pastor an Apostle's ministry. I should have known better. I wasn't involved with the finances, and I later learned that we were not paying for the building where the church was located. I was pastor there for a full year. We used the building free of charge, but the treasurer didn't save one dime during that time.

When I went to the Apostle's ministry, there was only one member. The assembly expanded under my guidance, and I took the new members with me when I left. Believe me, this was not an assembly split. There was nothing to split.

This is how the "Chosen By God" assembly came to be. Trust me, it was not my desire to start a ministry. All glory goes to Yahuah.

CHAPTER TEN
PIOUS

In the Bible, the word "pious" appears as "chasid." It means devout or godly. The problem is many people who try to appear to be pious are actually hypocrites.

In ancient Rome, a stage actor would wear a mask when playing different roles. People knew what it meant to be "two-faced." We still have plenty of two-faced people around today, but most of them are not actors. The only thing worse than being a hypocrite is when someone is a puppet with Satan pulling the strings, *John 8:44*. If that puppet also happens to be a pastor, then the devil is leading the assembly.

There are a few ways to tell when this is happening. First, the pastor does not practice what he preaches, *Matthew 23:3-4*. For example, there may be a pastor who is a millionaire and has a television show. He tells his assembly, "Trust God and send me a thousand dollars, and watch what He does for you." Well, if the pastor truly believes in that principle, he should say, "I trust God. So call me now, and I'll give you a thousand dollars."

Another thing these pastors do is make a big show of tithing. Sometimes they'll go as far as saying, "Will all the tithers please stand." This is very similar to the Pharisees who were known for praying in public, *Matthew 6:1-9*.

I know my wife loves me, and I don't get scared or jealous if a technician comes to my home while I'm away to hook up the cable. I'm confident. I'm not afraid of members of my ministry visiting other assemblies. If you're in a church where you have to get the pastor's permission to visit other churches, that's not respect. That is intimidation.

If your pastor has confidence in his teaching, then he should not be afraid of another pastor's influence. I don't threaten members of my assembly to get them to come every Sabbath. It's my teaching that keeps them coming back.

If your pastor does his/her research with a Bible dictionary instead of a Strong's Concordance, be careful. Yahusha and His disciples did not speak English. And if you're in a position where you feel like you can't question your pastor's teaching, you should RUN!

Popular preachers dance around issues concerning gays, Muslims, and unbelievers going to hell. People often misinterpret *Matthew 7:1*, "Judge not, that ye not be judged." Pastors use this as an excuse to bite their tongues rather than speak out against what is wrong. But the Bible gives you permission to evaluate someone's life, *Matthew 7:15-20*. If this was not true, then you would let your daughters date gang-bangers and your sons date prostitutes.

As a man of Yahuah, I must let you know if you're living in sin. I must tell you that you are going to hell if you don't know Yahusha. That's not judging; it's love. Remember, The Spirit grows good fruit – not bad fruit. Your fruit will make it clear who controls your life, Yahuah or Satan.

If your pastor only preaches prosperity, and he does not preach against sin, then you should look for somewhere else to go. We have to banish all Pharisee preachers.

Yahuah gave you free will, and it's time to make a choice. A worldly (money/prosperity) preacher is a satanic preacher, *1 John 2:15-17*. This is why they avoid passages like *Mark 10:25*, "It is easier for a camel to go through the eye of a needle, than for a rich man to enter into the kingdom of God."

People think I'm harsh for calling prosperity preachers satanic, but the Bible said it first, *James 4:3-4*. Praying in lust and being a friend of the world makes you an enemy of Yahuah.

You should also watch out for so-called "faith healers." If the only miracles you see performed by these people are in a church building, then common sense should tell you they are a fraud. The miracles performed by the Messiah were mostly done outside of an assembly building. The Holy Spirit should be found inside a person, not just a structure.

Whether you know it or not, witchcraft is being practiced in church buildings on a regular basis. These warlocks and witches are about control and domination. That spirit did not come from Yahuah.

Please remember that no one possesses the anointing. The anointing possesses you, so be wary of pastors who brag about powers they don't have, *James 4:6*. It's always better to talk less and let your works talk for you.

CONCLUSION

While I do believe that salvation is a heart issue, *Matthew 5:8*, I do not take light of His name, *Malachi 3:16-17*. If you go to school and ask, "Where is Mrs. Brooks' class?" someone will point you in the right direction. I don't believe that people praying in "Jesus'" name are wrong, but you should know what His name means. It will make your prayers much more powerful.

Watch out for Pharisees (preachers) who bully their flock. Watch out for the ones who are so passive and greedy for tithes, they allow their members to show up for worship half-naked. Watch out for preachers who want to be popular so badly, they're willing to sell their soul to Satan. Don't stone them with your tongue. You should pray for them. But the word never said you have to remain loyal to them.

I hear people say, "God has not spoken to me about leaving this church." The truth is God has not removed the scales from your eyes to allow you to see the falsehood in your pastor, *Acts 9:18*. I pray that one day He will show you the truth.

Literally, the New Testament means "new covenant," which is an agreement or contract. But please don't be fooled into believing the law by itself will save you. God has promised you eternal life, and He will not break His end of the agreement. But now that you know what the Pharisees are doing to corrupt you spiritually, you must make the right decisions so that you will keep your end of the agreement with God, *Ecclesiastes 12:13-14*.

    I will pray for your spiritual healing, and I will pray for my brothers and sisters still held in bondage by the pastors they look to for guidance. As for the Pharisees themselves, their days are numbered. They will soon have to face God and tell Him why they misled His flock. I would not like to be in their shoes when that day comes.

    May God bless you richly in grace and His presence. I give all glory and honor to Christ who is able to present us faultless before God, who is before all ages and eternal glory. Amein.

THE END
BY ELLIOTT BURNS

ABOUT THE AUTHOR

Elliott Burns was called to preach at 17 years of age. He has been going strong for 24 years. He was an assistant pastor at the age of 21. He has been shepherding God's people at his own assembly for 3 years. Elliott is an ordained minister. He can be contacted at *chosenbygod@msn.com*. Learn more about his ministry at *chosenbygod.vpweb.com*.

www.ingramcontent.com/pod-product-compliance
Lightning Source LLC
Chambersburg PA
CBHW031301290426
44109CB00012B/672